More Praise for *Shiny Things*

Shiny Things is a poetry collection that invites us to come and discover. Whether the subject is a bridge or damselfly, a post office or a painting, Michael Magee's rich observations and wonderfully startling comparisons coax us into seeing anew, listening again, rethinking, and reimagining. These deeply layered poems yield new meaning with each reading, and they are worth opening again and again.

—Connie Hampton Connally,
author of *Fire Music* and *The Songs We Hide*

SHINY
THINGS

SHINY THINGS

Michael Magee

MoonPath Press

Copyright © 2025 Michael Magee
All rights reserved.

No part of this publication may be reproduced, distributed, or transmitted in any form or by any means whatsoever without written permission from the publisher, except in the case of brief excerpts for critical reviews and articles. All inquiries should be addressed to MoonPath Press.

Poetry
ISBN 979-8-9899487-3-4

Cover Art: *Woman Playing the Cello*, Róbert Berény, 1928
Hungarian National Gallery, Budapest, Hungary

Interior Author Photo: Peter Scanlan
Back Cover Author Photo: Carl Palmer
transformed using NewProfilePic.com

Book design by Tonya Namura, using Gentium Book Basic

MoonPath Press, an imprint of Concrete Wolf Poetry Series,
is dedicated to publishing the finest poets
living in the U.S. Pacific Northwest.

MoonPath Press
c/o Concrete Wolf
PO Box 2220
Newport, OR 97365-0163

MoonPathPress@gmail.com

http://MoonPathPress.com

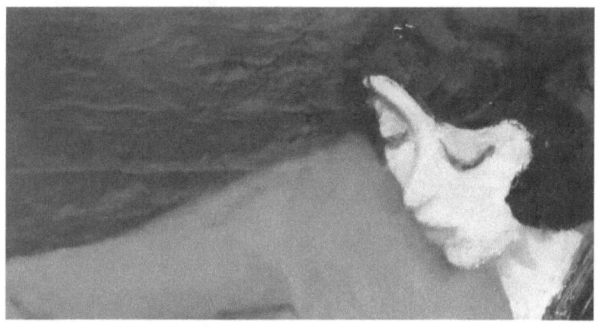

*To my cousin Donnie, who believes in cosmic tumblers,
my cousin Suzie, and other family gems.*

In Memoriam: Richard Blum

*To my dear friend and compatriot, age 80
1944–2024*

after George Herbert's "Easter Wings"

Tall and blue-eyed
your face a balm
joy and calm.

Truths self-evident
even in death, wearing
your pale egg-yellow T-shirt.

We rode together
on the bus, sidesaddle seats
mile after mile, always

the same smile, a knowing
look, ever the same,
a touch of the poet.

Espresso by the Bay, Steilacoom

for Michael Magee

by Peter Ludwin

As you recite your poem, Paris appears:
Proust sniffing the vapors of his cork-lined room
yields to a gallery in the Bohemian Quarter, to towers
    of books

at Shakespeare & Company. A way of life—the *only* life
    for those held thrall to word or stroke of brush.
The fertile dream of cobblestone mulched by moon.

And Steilacoom? The oldest settlement in Washington,
    an afterthought if thought about at all. Mere toad-
stool in the shadow of Tacoma, best known

for the state mental hospital I pass
    on the way into town. The stolid brick's
a trigger for terrors of Bedlam and electric shock,

those cells of filthy straw known to Monte Cristo
    whose keys a jailer threw away long ago.
Yes, Count, you cut quite the figure in your day,

but you're just another dung heap here. Ha! Ha!
    A large sign planted in the lawn hints
at the hidden costs behind those walls: *Hiring.*

But remembrance of things past pervades this
    coffeehouse,
    the dozen people cleansed by rain. Tumbling
into the Existential Café, Sartre argues with Camus,

flirts with de Beauvoir. How hungry people here are
  for such offerings, for nutrients
neither cable nor convenience store can give them.

Peter Ludwin is the recipient of a Literary Fellowship from Artist Trust, a winner of the Muriel Craft Bailey Memorial Award, and the 2024 winner of the Trail to Table Editors' Award in Poetry for *An Altar of Tides*.

TABLE OF CONTENTS

INTRODUCTION: *SHINY THINGS*   5

I   I HUGGED THE BRANDENBURG CONCERTO

I HUGGED THE BRANDENBURG CONCERTO #2	9
TO BE IN BUDAPEST	10
SOLILOQUY 141, A MINOR TIME WASTED	11
DEPARTURE	12
EVENTIDE	13
WILL SHEEP SAFELY GRAZE	14
HOLDING ON IN IRPIN, UKRAINE	15
BUDAPEST COUPLETS	17
BUDAPEST AFTER DARK	18
THE LIGHTED BRIDGES OF BUDAPEST	19
WHAT I DISCOVERED DURING COVID	20
FIUMEI CEMETERY, BUDAPEST	21
F1	22
MILLEFIORI	23

II   PRO FEMINA

LIPSTICK	27
EVE	29
THE DOLLS	30
AUDREY HEPBURN AND THE CAT WITH LUMINOUS EYES IN THE GARAGE	31
DORIAN GRAY	32
MR. CANNOLI, CALICO CAT	33
I AM A FILM ACTRESS	34
STOLEN MOMENTS	35
DAMSELFLY	36
GOLDEN-CROWNED KINGLETS	37
WINTER KALE	38
SONG FOR A YOUNG TOWNSEND'S WARBLER, MALE	39
FOR CRUMBS	40

WOMAN WITH A BIRDCAGE	41
WOMAN WITH A CELLO RED DRESS	42
A CUBIST MAN READING HIS NEWSPAPER	43
THE PAINTER AND HIS MODEL	44
SADIE AND HER SCISSORS	45
TO THE KOREAN HAIRDRESSER ON OUR POETRY WALK	46
ONLY SON	47
EASTER LILY	48
I DO THE TANGO AT THE AWP	49
DURGA'S DREAM	50
THE VOICE IN THE MACHINE	51

III SHINY THINGS

VAN GOGH IN LONDON	55
PRICK MY THUMB	57
THROUGHOUT THE BODY, THANKFULLY	58
THIS LIME-TREE BOWER, MY PASSION	59
BLACKPOOL	61
FLOTSAM	62
BY-THE-WIND SAILORS	63
TWIN HARBORS STATE PARK, NEAR GRAYLAND	64
NACHES TAVERN	65
VISITING HAWORTH, TOP WITHENS	66
OF HUMANS	68
DR. SUN YAT-SEN GARDEN: KOI DELIBERATIONS	69
MODERN SURREALISM	71
THE LOVE LETTER	72
POST OFFICE	73
POSTA	74
NIGHT MAILMAN	75
SILENCE WAS DEAFENING	76
COSMONAUTS	77

RADAR EYE	78
CROSSING TO NOWHERE	79
ROCK CARVINGS:	
CHINESE RECONCILIATION SHRINE	
TACOMA, WASHINGTON	80
OTTO'S SONG	82
ELEVATOR	83
FIELDS OF COLOR	84
BIRTHDAY CARD	85
LIMBO	86
EXHIBITION IN BUDAPEST,	
SZÉPMŰVÉSZETI MÚZEUM	87
GOLD MEDAL	88
SUMMER IS LIGHT TO THE TOUCH	89
SHINY THINGS	90
ACKNOWLEDGMENTS	91
ABOUT THE AUTHOR	93

SHINY THINGS

*No special purpose in mind concerning the decorations,
simply the outcome of a moment, an inspirational diversion.*
>   —Anton Kamp, *"John Singer Sargent as
>   I Remember Him"*

All I want is a poem that sings.
>   —Diana Hendry

INTRODUCTION: *SHINY THINGS*

> *The sound of her singing was something like a cello getting up in the morning.*
> —Richard Goldstein, about the German singer Nico on the album *The Velvet Underground & Nico*.

Michael Magee has lived in England and traveled widely, but calls the Northwest home. In October 2023, he traveled to Budapest and crossed many bridges, leading to the chapbook *Budapest After Dark*, published in 2024 by Open Sesame Books. Section I of *Shiny Things* reflects those travels. In Section II, "Pro Femina," his mother, late wife, cats, movie stars, and paintings come into play. Section III explores the natural world, and inner and outer landscapes from earth and space.

This collection is a map without a compass to guide you. Start wherever "shiny things" appear in your eye, as you cross bridges from Pest into the hills of Buda, or in the reflections of portrait artists: Sargent, Berény, Van Gogh, Rippl-Rónai, and Vermeer. Michael also draws music from the wells of Bach, Liszt, Oliver Nelson, and Astor Piazzolla. And yes, from the cello, that most passionate and sensuous of instruments (besides the voice), one that you can get your arms around.

I

I HUGGED THE BRANDENBURG CONCERTO

Antal's bow danced over the strings until the very air sang.
　　—Connie Hampton Connally,
　　　The Songs We Hide

I HUGGED THE BRANDENBURG CONCERTO #2

I hugged the Brandenburg Concerto #2
put my arms around the horn section put
the flute of your mouth to mine held the
strings of your bra, bowed against you
while I loved each burst of sound
touching your hand to stroke you
hair brushing your hair with my thumbs.
The baton of my hand bringing you along
as you laughed at each new invention
playing arpeggios up and down the scale
along your arm. Then you dozed during
the piano until the sound of your hum
reverberated on my cheek a sounding
board for the finale knowing the way we
bond—I hugged
the Brandenburg Concerto in my bare
arms.

TO BE IN BUDAPEST

Crossing bridges,
the Danube from Buda to Pest
where I can see both sides of life
the Citadel after the Conquest
a heron in a treetop

I come to Margit Island
in the middle, following a path
past the gelato stand and fountain
into the wood, a coffee plant
from Brazil growing free red berries.

And at an old oak tree romancing
the crown, canopy leafing like a monarchy
from all those Hungarian kings
when I pause, a butterfly nurses
a dandelion in the breeze.

I come to the statue of a man who
like Cyrano de Bergerac penned
from Rostand, with an overflowing
cape who invites me onto his lap
like a child to be told.

On a grassy lawn, dreaming up stories
that carry me to the North Sea
on multicolored tulip wings of a
hot-air balloon over Városliget Park
into the sunset at the other end.

SOLILOQUY 141, A MINOR TIME WASTED

In the great time of condominiums
if we don't look down.
In the time of radioactive isotopes
punch lines from old songs and tropes

we are ready to unwind this morning,
the shuttered decks are empty
as icing on a bridal cake
decorations to be eaten later.

So, I mistake artifice for invention
seems to me an old e-melody
yet to be played on YouTube or
elsewhere, people appear

on the balcony to deliver soliloquies
to seagulls who make their exits
and cars queuing up to leave
the freeway below the radiant blue

of somewhere in the long hereafter
unattainable before we had come
to build our monuments in concrete,
plaster, giving way to art nouveau.

And the replication of human genomes.
So, we repeat ourselves, once again.

DEPARTURE

This morning I let the gray gristle
of rain cover my cheeks
and as I wheeled my baggage
onto the tram, everyone looked sad.

At the bus stop two men
dressed in black like a cortege
accompanied me
as though I needed bodyguards.

Once I reached Departures
I followed the line that snaked
into the underground parking lot
where I found a Visa card.

Turned it in at the checkpoint,
a refugee from America
on my way to Budapest, where
the sky opened like a suitcase.

EVENTIDE

This evening comes early
in the fog of peace
here in Tacoma, far away
from Gaza, the Middle East.

I doze on the couch
a refugee from Budapest,
a tired traveler who rests
against an embroidered pillow.

Not a coronation mantle
silk restitched by Queen Zita
in its beautiful afterlife, now
under glass beneath fingertips.

I retrace, following
the patterns as I do the trees
this evening in this haze—
blanketing us, topography of

different worlds, linked together
into chains that bridge
Buda and Pest, we walk across
from Hungarian to English.

Where the river flows south then
east through Romania, Serbia
and on to the Black Sea, where
Russians have been bombing Kyiv.

WILL SHEEP SAFELY GRAZE

Away from gunfire, mortar shells
Israeli bombardment—
turning meadows into headstones,
craters, churning earth into sea.
How to deliver us from assaults
on our senses as we see through
our rectangular vision the tanks
that trample our fields, the infantry
of camouflage that tries to hide
where there is no refuge, O give us
safe haven, a place to graze
far from here where the
hare is not in their crosshairs
and the earth is not a firing range
and we are not target practice for
soldiers who Netanyahu sends
to scorch our homes, tear up
our flocks who after all are here
only to protect the shepherds.

HOLDING ON IN IRPIN, UKRAINE

response to the April 7, 2022, photo and article by Tim Judah in the <u>New York Review of Books</u>

As I watch those people
crossing the wooden plank
in Irpin trying to escape
under the concrete bridge
catching their collective breath
egged on by soldiers to cross

the rushing river with plastic
bags and knapsacks, carrying
their food, being led like children
to cross the current, the disabled
the elderly, the lame, the weak
of heart as Russian drones
home in to attack them as targets
I think what do I have to fear?

My neighborhood break-ins,
homeless camps, hot-wiring
the ignition, broken glass, but
really, no *Kristallnacht* to speak of
the piling up of trash and plastic
is nothing compared to continuous
shelling, missile barrages, intense
artillery all around them.

As they cross the wooden bridge
to escape while a soldier holds a
woman's hand above as though
they're dancing a minuet—

to be stopped at any moment by
a shell, a missile, a gunshot
to rip their fragile dance apart.

BUDAPEST COUPLETS

You're on the same line
that holds you together

after the split chin, the blood
you spilled on the pavement

what you left in Budapest
that made you understood

by the doctor who spoke no
English except "Will you lie down?"

You suffer the paper cuts
as you feel the bite of needles.

Each one hurts like a poem.
Each one a slice of life

hurts to the bone, but makes
you hold your breath's caesura.

That stings as you write down
what no one can name

except in a moment of *piano*
as you try to heal in poems.

BUDAPEST AFTER DARK

At night I look out from my window
across the square, where Romany gather
to banter and dogs bark to the sound
of a harmonica as skateboards form a rhythm
section and people from the tavern are toasting
half-moon glasses while I am dry tonight here—

in the cell of my room more monkish than Kafka
although there are bars on our doors, I hear
singing and across the city, I can see lights
from the Margit Bridge as a white halo appears
while above small lights appear in clusters—
constellations in the hills of Buda, make
lovely ornaments for those of us in Pest.

THE LIGHTED BRIDGES OF BUDAPEST

The lighted bridges of Budapest
    like Byzantine birds and mosaics,
    Constantine, Theodora, their entourage
    and I plain in face, wide-eyed
    face their presence in the East.

I walk along the strand of the Duna
    coveting my days and nights
    the ones I walked over at sunset
    each one calling its name.
    Margit, Erzsébet, Széchenyi, Liberty.

Linked together into chains
    that bridge Buda and Pest
    I translate across from Hungarian
    to English, the days to come
    spelled out in lights like holy braille.

WHAT I DISCOVERED DURING COVID

Tiny daisies that close at night
the damselfly lying on one side
the greens of the park
that deepened like my iris
waving a pinhole of my existence
that turned inside out.

The sky took a beat like I
was counting stars on a string
that played along my hand
twisting the lines into spider
webs that met in the center
of my palm, a place to hide and dream.

FIUMEI CEMETERY, BUDAPEST

Never had a place felt so dead
the smell of death was in the air
chestnuts exploding all around me
dropping from the sky, a sarcophagus
in repose, a mausoleum foreclosed
the wrought iron fence seemed to be
holding hands through the long colonnade
I imagined gravestones nodding heads.

Poets were there and artists too,
a photographer's exhibit set up
black slate plates, Klösz, György
I thought of Robert Capa, how he died
stepping on a land mine and watched
my feet, thought of his mother grieving
at his grave. They died in stone,
veined marble Deák, Ferenc,
the photo of the gymnasium in 1905
where ice skaters go hand in hand
and little girls turn into swans.

A chapel to play in, an open door
to all who come here to find peace
dance in circles of the leaves,
turn their sails to the wind
that blows through Fiumei to rest,
a man plays his lute decorated on
a crypt, children, flowers in their laps
form a wreath to surround him in.
A place of peace rooted in the earth.

F1

She muses the passing
of her husband,
her arms embrace
a vessel of the state.

Yet, her view remains
of what's reflected here
his name at her fingertips.

Where she in white
like the moon, one side
in light, one in darkness.

MILLEFIORI

Here in blossoms that spill onto the long-necked
wavering bursts of iris-waving handkerchiefs
and fields of tulips that would touch us
with their lips if it was only allowed.

Dripping nests of amethyst, Austin roses,
cinnabar, magenta, pale white mercury,
narcissus yellow and green sword fern
remind us of how our retina attaches
to the cones and rods in our own iris.

How we wander, still unable to touch,
but still feeling swayed by the overtones
as though glass-blowing had fired in us
our frozen liquid poses into reflecting shapes
rounding our corners into one continuous being.

From the sweating hot shop to the rapture of
the gallery, a chosen chorus of flowers
raising their heads above ours to cheer, instead
this ornamental view of the universe
washing down our palates' holy grail.

Awaken the many words, we jump between
like lily pads, ready to see for ourselves
the eye as it beholds these garden gods.

II

PRO FEMINA

To be fully alive, fully human, and completely awake is to be continually thrown out of the nest.
    —Pema Chödrön

It is fascinating that the modern female personality permeates even the old-fashioned historist milieu fashioned in anticipation of the great female types of the twentieth century.
    —Museum Guide, Hungarian National Gallery,
     about the painter Károly Lotz
     Germany 1833–Budapest 1904

LIPSTICK

> *World's oldest known lipstick found in Iran.*
> —<u>The Washington Post</u>

From Mesopotamia and Iran
in the bad old Bronze Age days
it might have been applied
with a brush, at first blush
it was an intense red
with "hematite," Greek word
for blood, exactly what you'd
expect in a modern lipstick!

In a vial with an evil eye
carbon-dated to 1936 (BC) that is
pre–Gloria Swanson, Williams
Holden and Wilder, *Sunset Boulevard*
like a marsh cane in appearance
"the dead wore it and the living too!"
adorned young Egyptians in Haute Cuisine
Dynasty who with brush eye-liner
adored themselves in the mirror.

In the Rustic Era, pre-Elizabethan
Elizabeth Taylor, and her consort
Richard Burton, a.k.a., à la Cleopatra
pre-exploration of other continents
and the explorer Sir Richard Burton, too.
Before the Nile was discovered
a source of pre-denialists when
dental dams were built, think Aswan
before Rommel and the Dogs of WWII

Puabi was first to apply it
Queen before Freddie Mercury

and ABBA, red rocks and rouge
rose to her lips of fame and Little
Richard found "Good Golly, Miss Molly"
days, Sumerians and Egyptians all used it.
Anointing the lips before lip-lock
then, came nail polish and the world
was astonished once again.

EVE

after the sculpture by George Tsutakawa

She hugs herself
before it all began
a woman alone curled
into herself, her hand
around her breast
progenitress, but
at loose ends, huddled
there without words
before there was a need
for communion.

I think of her dark
cedar body made from
burl and wonder how she
came to be the woman
that we know, a part
of the tree we know as life
that cradles her still
the pebbled green—
her great dark spirit
wrapped around her
like a wound, a serpent
she can never escape.

THE DOLLS

The dolls are all dressed up
in crinoline, with Goldilocks curls.
The dolls are waiting to take their vows
with ribbons; they are being prepped,
the ballerina dolls *en pointe*, ankles bound
like Chinese girls, feet pared into slippers
doing *relevés* and *pliés*; release them soon.

For they are caught, even broad-brimmed dolls
who look like Scarlett O'Hara, waiting
to descend the long staircase to Rhett Butler,
dolls who are ready to take communion or
be admitted to convent schools are praying,
tears welling up in their angel eyes,
with rubbery arms and dimpled smiles.

As they dance to their hurt heels,
some are going to church, or are rehearsing
for choir practice; some even sing in cages,
like Marie Antoinette, sway from their perches.
Who will pull their chains? No one will
help them, these sad-eyed doe-eyed dolls,
of daydreams, starving for affectionate hugs.

Tear-stained, the dolls are all dolled-up,
and no one is going to take them home; no one
will marry the extra-virgin dolls. They
are still waiting to grow up, won't you please
save the dolls now; take them home by their
waxen hands; help them to stand up on
their own two feet, so they can walk alone
or until men who are real dolls come along.

AUDREY HEPBURN AND THE CAT WITH LUMINOUS EYES IN THE GARAGE

She tried to sit in my lap while I was standing up
—Philip Marlowe in <u>The Big Sleep</u>

It stares from the concrete walls
wearing a diamond choker.
A little bit of Lucy in the Sky,
Audrey with her cigarette holder.

The cat dressed up in white
like a flyweight boxer in the ring
or the cover of a Raymond Chandler
novel in bas-relief, while Audrey poses

a stencil of a pencil in black stiletto dress.
And heels, Audrey's pipestem legs
at your service and the cat
tucked nicely on her lap while she's

standing up so thin that no one
even the cat can tell the difference
as she steals in the door sideways
for a breakfast at Tiffany's.

DORIAN GRAY

Prowls the neighborhood late at night
looking for his reflection in the window,
shrinks from sight, his shadow, gray
with white paws, a trail of London Fog.

That clothes him, just a whiff of cat cologne
a sense of *dangereuse*, a velvet curse
his glassy eye sees through itself
to the other side of wonderment.

Out at night, a bowl of milk, late-night
snacks among the neighborhood riffraff
catch-as-catch-can or can't, who can deny
the nine lives he's spent, trying to escape

his fate as Dorian Gray will never rest
until he's found and lost himself at last.

MR. CANNOLI, CALICO CAT

Black-and-white Calico—
a fur-collar wrap around his neck
like the spiral nebula itself.

Walks on the right side
of the street, every doorway
a nook and cranny to nap in the sun.

The accountant keeps track of him,
the toy store, Tricky's
with treats and handouts.

Every planter a sandbox with
the warm smell of urine,
and every flower a friend.

To whomever is listening in—
a kind word, a helping hand,
cat's collar, black-and-white socks.

Mr. Cannoli, a touch of the poet
keeps his feet dry, counts his blessings
one mouse at a time.

I AM A FILM ACTRESS

In my blank verse my face is furtive
still sleeping in, semi-wide-awake
I try to read my lines in coffee grounds hoping
for a dash of *savoir-faire* and snakes
that wind around my little fingernail
as I age gracefully into middle age.

There is no word for the kind of kind word
to lay bare my inner *sang-froid*, a chill
is in the air, it may be my *film noir*
complex acting up looking for a broken dream
or two, or better yet, a nightmare still
frozen like a Garbo statue or Gene Tierney
with her highly modeled cheekbones, à la *Laura*
in waiting for her secret detective to appear.

STOLEN MOMENTS

inspired by composer Oliver Nelson

What more could you take or thieve?
The liquid coronet, the steady pulse of the bass
a pooling piano playing its water music?

Fluttering at the window a breathy voyeur
filling the branches with trills, dripping faucet
from the alto sax giving its marinated vibe.

Eric Dolphy, his dolphin-beat playing behind
    Bill Evans
throwing in two cents' worth, rippling the keyboard.
Then, reprise of horns with a chill breeze, *sang-froid*.

DAMSELFLY

I haven't changed my spots yet
but here my testament stands.
I am a damselfly who passes
before your eyes as an insect.

Sleeping on one side, one wing
open, rising, and my filament
I can't change my skin
that breaks out into sunspots.

I try to keep myself awake
covering my daydreams in a waking
blanket, body thin as a pencil
ready to write down with feeling.

My fingers light to the touch
my own transparent life—
dead or alive don't change
your spots for anything or anyone!

GOLDEN-CROWNED KINGLETS

Little golden-crowned kinglets in
the fir trees flash gold as leaves
in their cameo roles.

Today there was snow in the air
small patches of light that
brushed against my jacket.

What's best? The little flash
of a kinglet that moves so fast
it leaves behind its color.

Or this snow-fleeting day
coming out of nowhere to appear
at my side like a sunflower.

WINTER KALE

in memory of my wife, Jean

When limbs had all
come down with morning glory
askew I came looking for *you*.

Where masonry crumbled
on the wall and concrete cracked
I wondered what I lacked.

To find you, over the bridge
of sighs and the prevailing breeze
splinters of light appeared.

I came to a garden spot
with globes of winter kale
made into a sphere.

Taken from an Escher print
and felt the thrill of
discovering you *here*.

SONG FOR A YOUNG TOWNSEND'S WARBLER, MALE

With your bright mustard-yellow
vest, you're a rogue alright.
Black stripe wraparound pansy face
green shining arrow down
the middle of your back
that "feathered" touch of flight.

You stand out from the pack.
I can still see flashes of yellow
ringing the black *maschera*
radiating all around you, V-neck
pullover, cutting quite a figure
waiting for your date, perhaps.

FOR CRUMBS

Little sparrows
puffed up sidewalk *boulevardiers*
make their way among tables
shadows of the streets of Paris
awnings protrude, but little sparrows
are the truth of what we eat.

Making their way among the waiters
and croissants, they shine best
in daylight through the end of
our glasses raising a toast to them
true fame among the crumbs we
have left them.

WOMAN WITH A BIRDCAGE

after the painting by József Rippl-Rónai, 1892,
Magyar Nemzeti Galéria, Budapest

She sings to us
through pouting lips,
her back arched, eyes
averted in pale white,
a chocolate cocktail dress.

The cage is green
and she holds it
as if it was a lantern
casting out its spell
of musical notes.

Where we will hear
nothing but what she sees,
a bird in twilight,
she in a trance of ultraviolet
green glowing aurora borealis.

WOMAN WITH A CELLO
RED DRESS

after the painting by Róbert Berény

Legs splayed like a starfish
she practices her cello
wide octopus shoulders, arms extend
like she is embracing a reef,
holding its circumference tight.

The breadth of cello
extends from her chest
to the floor where it is anchored
there and her red dress
surrounds her like a tide.

From below, like sonar through bubbles
go to the surface, her head
like a diver's helmet,
her deep-sea expression summons,
vibrations of her diving bell.

A CUBIST MAN READING HIS NEWSPAPER

To Be Read Down   *Or Across*

He holds it up in two hands	the crossword's checkerboard
one on either side	in black and white, missing teeth
creased in the middle world	a gap-toothed crooked grin.
The sun of his bald head shines	his head disappearing for now
above the paper stiff	behind a cloud, it darkens
and bending to his will	going down beneath the fold
an origami—in progress;	but at times peering out at me
cutting with his fingers	as I in my quiet way, read him
makes it into a cross	he claps his hands and stares
drawn and quartered at the fold	over his glasses, just the man
like the bridge of his nose	pensively surveys the page
slightly out of joint	a map of the world, still flat.

THE PAINTER AND HIS MODEL

after the painting by Károly Ferenczy,
Magyar Nemzeti Galéria, Budapest

He takes her hand
as though dancing a minuet
twists it into position
while turning his back to us
the model keeps her head erect
while he moves away to leave
her on her pedestal in space.

Just as I pick up a pen to write
this poem, leaving behind
my cozy chair for these four
corners framed in white to fit
my subject, fingers used to shape
what I hope once I drop the brush
will stand on its own.

SADIE AND HER SCISSORS

The stars aren't safe around her
not to mention a paper moon
she gives her blessings to,
the Big Dipper spills its cream
fresh from cows and Sadie
cutting away in paper chains
a smiling Venus girl dazzles
rectangles, squares, turning
to diagonals, gables, roof lines.
Gothic spires, Romanesque arches
turn upside down on their sides
a snow globe of golden domes
Ottoman Empires, architecture
of paper cuts, assembling, reassembling
the sky so it never comes down.

TO THE KOREAN HAIRDRESSER ON OUR POETRY WALK

Come out of the river
dry your long strands
mixed with kimchee
as she combs you out
among the chickadees
flitting among red alders.

Your mane is black and shiny
as raven's wings
and you in the crossbeak
of scissors, for here
there are no predators
but a rush along the creek.

As we stop to read a poem
letting it sink in
like the little slug who
glistened, listen to
the snip, snip of what's left
of your poetic wet ends.

ONLY SON

My mea culpas are all done
having forgiven myself
as an only son
I have nothing left to hide
or add to the gene pool.
But the ABCs of elementary
school, the arithmetic
of love and Galileo—
Pythagorean theorems
are hot within my blood.

The shell of a half-moon
waits above to be polished off.
There are only holes in the
ozone layer. I can't confess
my past. Only children figure
in my future, the chimes of wind songs
the solitary tongues
of shoes left in the doorway where
no woman waits for my whistle.

EASTER LILY

for Leona Magee, 1911–1994

Its twin white crowns
    bow a little,
like you did once,
and the spine curves.

One blossom refuses
to open as the sun
comes around lighting
    up your name.

It's a soft place
I sit on in the grass,
the Easter egg hunts
are all over by now.

I reserve this as
my nesting ground with
its latticelike squares,
that make a necklace.

The chick in your eggshell
locket I buried you in
must have popped open by
now, no longer fledgling.

I think of you there
in your white pine box
your hands crossed
no eggs left to hatch.

I DO THE TANGO AT THE AWP

NO DANCING

No dancing in the elevator,
social distancing is preferred,
don't tango, even without a partner
you will be observed.

Among the bookstalls we bob and weave
in crossover steps, 1-2-3-4; then open the door
as she *grapevines* around my open position
while I do a box step we're finding our form
as people stop to thank us: "You look great."
Yes, because it's been so long since Covid
brought us to a halt, our histories stopped
we tried to carry on, but no one cared enough!

Now we're free again in the vast dance hall
of the Northwest Convention Center, among
the runways to move once more to find our way
in serpentine ways among the warm bodies,
just a *walking step* to take us away again to when
the tango stopped as hand on back, she follows me
whichever step I choose among the book covers' spines
crossover, check step, open the door as we glide
in socks, a perfect couple once more, slightly off
but in style, doing signature *ochos* across the floor.

DURGA'S DREAM

She drove from New York City,
five days cross-country, alone,
talked to truckers on a CB.

Went to the truck stops not knowing
any better, she was young and innocent
with a car filled with jars of honey.

She studied yoga, a voice from a swami
guided her, filled her head with chants,
drove her all the way to the West Coast.

Clear to California, a car full of bees
that never stung for love nor money,
she cruised across the Bay Bridge.

Then on to San Francisco, laughed
all the way to the Tenderloin District,
had a good time settling in.

At the end of the streetcar line
Hyde and Beach, the Buena Vista Café
where it makes its turnaround—

She set up her home, flirted
like a moth with strobe lights, danced
like a sugar cube in an Irish coffee.

THE VOICE IN THE MACHINE

As a child I used to sing "Be My Love"
as though I was Mario Lanza—
hiding behind the living room sofa
to serenade my parents in my childish tenor.
And with my kisses set you burning
straining for the highest notes, trying
to be true to the voice of the master or
whoever else would listen, *that I adore.*

All the while the Capitol dome on the label
kept spinning around in the background
with a purple sky I wanted to fly around
until I was too dizzy for love of the record
machine in my voice to turn it off; and it
kept spinning like the wheel of fortune until
I knew, *eternally—that you—will be my love!*

III

SHINY THINGS

Between grasp and reach,
between this shiny object and that dull thing.
—Sati Mookherjee, "Mind the Gap!"

VAN GOGH IN LONDON

*"We are all In the gutter,
but some of us are looking at the stars."*
    —Oscar Wilde, Lady Windermere's Fan

His Dutch accent in guttural cadence
ordering fish and chips
trying to take it in, walking
along the Thames, reflections
of the chestnut trees with
yellow leaves then strolling
through Soho with its red lights,
no tulips tied in ribbons.

His prehistory from primordial sludge
the wattle and daub school
of painting, his writer's pen obeys him
better than his brush, his love
of life from Charles Dickens's charcoal
and soot, in South London he knew
Tooting and Clapham Common
as he made his Pilgrim's Progress.

O starry night, O northern lights
he walks in writer's boots
through London, the poor in harness,
potato-eaters of the earth, mutton
and gruel, he shares a table
at an eel house in Peckham with
green liquor on his mash, piled high
as haystacks, then down the dark
roads back to his room.

Before the haystacks and the doorsteps
before the poverty and foresight
that led him south to Arles,
Van Gogh like a cough spread his life
laying down the weight of his bedroll,
in thick strokes that came
as he wandered the hamlets to stoke
his soul, trade his bread for art.

PRICK MY THUMB

after reading David Moolten's "Cézanne's Diabetes"

I, too, have pricked my skin
followed the glucose meter readings that
look like Fahrenheit and Celsius temperatures
depending on how my day has been.

Suffered the peaks and valleys
and found that I have more calluses
than a sparring partner. But it all adds up
somehow when you're trying to negotiate

what sweet thing to eat next or
the amount of sugar I put in my coffee
or whether I should exercise more
in the mirror after looking at myself.

Who would know that a "thin man" like
myself has to battle against the ropes
as the doctor checks my feet to see if
I can feel what's at the end of my leg,

that I know too well, diverging out into
the hinterlands of my extremities where
it's often cold, or too hot with my own blood
to know when I'm on a sugar high instead.

I, too, have pricked my thin skin
used the needle's shiny compass
blue veins like arterials on a road map
to see what's at the other end.

THROUGHOUT THE BODY, THANKFULLY

Found poem, Doctor's notes

Biopsy of the right forearm
showed a melanoma in situ.
This is a skin cancer that
needs to be treated as there
is a risk that it can spread.

Throughout the body, thankfully
the lesion is limited (like my poetry)
to the top layer of the skin
and a wide local excision in
Dermatology will likely be curative.

Our team will reach out to you
to schedule you for excision.

   A Right Forearm

THIS LIME-TREE BOWER, MY PASSION

after Samuel Taylor Coleridge's
"This Lime-Tree Bower My Prison"

How I have looked at you
through the windows of the conservatory
your round ripe fruit, orbs
hanging like Escher globes
what words I hold on these lines.
My lines can only amplify your
circles, the fullness of your prism.

In my home, my friends are all
long-distance now, I only hear them
across these heart-shaped lines
I share with you—that touch my hands.
How I would wonder about them
among the pine needles in the park
the sun has gone—daylight saving
time has ended.

I am left with this darkness, although
I see the moon hanging like an earring from
a lobe I cannot see, except Jupiter and Saturn
are in conjunction for that brief time, a double planet
and I am alone with beauty's sense
of loss—my friends are at arm's length
now because of social distancing.

I mourn their long-ago egos, am left
with this lime-tree bower, my prism
would like to visit them in their hollows
and rooms, as I am here in warmth
but under the dripping eave I take

refuge from my poem. Yes, my poem.
And your poem too, which I share with you.

I am left-handed with only this lime-tree
bower in the conservatory, can only press
my face against the glass thinking
of them each in their apartments, homes
tucked in—but in this lime-tree bower
my passion, I would like to break the glass
pluck just one and peel its skin for my Cuba libre
to celebrate the freedom for which, my gentle friends
I share this glass half-empty.

BLACKPOOL

Helicopters fly in from the oil rigs
and you can hear the Irish Sea
preaching on its dimpled shore.

And the long line of the horizon
where two silhouettes stand pointing
out across the water flat

as a carpenter's level, you can
watch the storms come in and go
out again, there's a hole in the sky

for the sun to shine through
and the giant Ferris wheels around
sweeps you up and down again.

The sandstone steps like waterfalls
along the beached detritus and jetsam
pull you into where no-man's-land

is a tidal pool, begins the black kelp,
old socks wash up, the sky above
the Isle of Man buttery at sunset as toast.

Over there is Ireland,
somewhere beyond the mind's imagining
eye and the tram rumbles its way.

Pat's Bingo is calling the shots
and mermaids are hanging from
the light poles, dancing.

Toward Cleveleys Bay as the dark clouds
roll on, a man walked out of his tennis
shoes and was never seen again.

FLOTSAM

On the shore as Long Beach
stretches under a common sign of
sand, a strand of beach unwinds
left by the ocean, land's end waves.

Come home to roost from Japan,
debris from Fukushima nuclear reactors
washing up, tenpenny nails
tentacles from an octopus and all

the messages in bottles left to open
iron rust, barnacles break
the backs of rocks, and split
crab legs too black to eat.

And still we find purse seiners' nets
splinters of wood from packing crates
unpacked and left to drift, a circle
left from Dante's *Purgatorio*.

As he crossed the River Styx
a life preserver, and life raft floats
from shipwrecked ships washed up
from the mouth of the Columbia.

Shall we sing like Homer in the *Odyssey*
and look for heroes yet to come
striding like a Colossus along the boardwalk
carrying a starfish in our arms.

BY-THE-WIND SAILORS

They look like blue mussels
translucent fins catch the light
they wash up piled high
like little amphibious haystacks
drifting along the beach
with poisonous tentacles
that can't reach you—
who are detached to them.

Distant relations to jellyfish,
they move by coastal winds
stranded on the beach—
like tourists who have stayed
too long, waiting for a strong
wind and current to move on
down the shoreline, for bars
to open, happy hours to begin.

TWIN HARBORS STATE PARK, NEAR GRAYLAND

Signs for cannabis and sea views.
If you have cannabis you don't need one.
A busker plays "An English Garden"
outside of Aberdeen on his violin.

I follow the slough of the road
past the Ocean Spray cranberry bog
and over the bridge where oysters

are sleeping and shells pile up
where water is washing at my feet,
a gooeyduck on a roadside sign.

Razor clams waiting to be dug.
Mushrooms are for compost,
clam guns on the porch.

I make a foxhole in the sand
hollow out a place and burrow
like a butter clam. Here—

there are no words for winds
that move around where I sink
in my wormhole, brace myself

and work my way down away
from speech while waves recoil
keep moving me offshore.

As continents pull away the tide
is pushing back trying to keep
me from floating clear to Asia.

NACHES TAVERN

for Allen Braden

On the wall were the horns of hunters,
antlers of deer and elk mounted
in 3D effect with furry backgrounds.

Five-prong "beauties," fishing poles, and creels
tucked in a corner in the tavern
where we were the wooden nickels.

Out back, a barbecue pit,
blackened charcoal and the pines and firs
were cordoned off with chicken wire.

A chain-link fence kept us in the compound
among towering firs and cedars,
interlopers trying to get in as freeloaders.

Meanwhile, they pounded out hamburgers,
baskets of fries and baked beans
and filled us with soda and beer.

I looked at the cabin walls, thought of
Stewart Granger standing in his wellies
Trader Horn, King Solomon's Mines

imagining the open-mouthed heads
of big-game hunters, all ready and waiting
to be mounted by their trophy wives.

VISITING HAWORTH, TOP WITHENS

after Jane Satterfield's "Haworth of Other Days"

When I went the clouds were lowering
the stones were terse
the heath bleak as my verse.

I walked the winding streets
as my shoes cobbled the road.
Everything needed polish I thought.

I was spitting Yorkshire pudding
the wind blew me inside out, a few
guttural greetings from my chest.

I walked toward Top Withens, looking
for Cathy, finding ruins, what did
I expect: a bunch of bleating sheep?

But a wedding was in progress
in town, black coats, white veils
plenty of Nottingham lace.

As the bride vanished into a hearse
I walked alone to the graveyard,
never a trace of Heathcliff or Cathy.

Just as the mists closed in ghostly
at the Brontës' front door, I heard
cloven hooves of the passing tourists.

White veils, black morning coats,
a trail of flowers, I walked alone
under an undertaker's sky.

In the cemetery, the sound of footsteps
going away, leaving me forever
in stone words of the churchyard.

Made my way toward the station, down
the switchback hill toward the Worth Valley,
worthless melancholy of each footstep.

OF HUMANS

Where the scent went cold,
an encampment, lighter fluid
where someone cooked, warmed
himself in the slow decease.

All remains are human
I think this morning where
I pat out a fire in the woods
a campground, left over.

Ruins nearby, a charred grill
grown still, sending up mixed
smoke signals, messages rising
puffs of soot as if someone

had been burning documents
instead of sonnets, traces
of what is left behind to hold dear,
a new whole to fill the earth.

DR. SUN YAT-SEN GARDEN: KOI DELIBERATIONS

This morning in Dr. Sun Yat-Sen
Garden I hold quiet deliberations
"Keep Calm and Carry On."

I write among the bamboo
and limestone without fossil
fuel, I drink coffee and eat

a pineapple bun from around
the corner at Goldstone's Bakery
and once inside find a haven.

Outside, as the crow flies,
the statue of the good doctor
presides at the entrance

while I take my place in nature
by a peaceable kingdom, sit
like a toadstool among birdsong.

In April, a harbor seal got inside
flopped up Main Street from
the harbor and took his fill of koi.

Now they're back again, flipping
their golden tails in the yin and yang
while I take up my inner space.

And everything is safe and balanced
as I stand in the pagoda, looking
out across the rippling pond to walk

across the little bridge to the island
as a man would walk across the water
from mainland China to Taiwan

to see in his reflection if he is saved.
And so I pass among the shrines
as he did among the peasants, the good

doctor with his vision of a new China
thinking of my own revolution to come,
overtaking the new dynasties of age.

MODERN SURREALISM

To go from Sun Yat-Sen
in 1912 to contemporary surrealism
is a culture leap like Jonah's
out-of-the-body-of-a-whale
experience, the room's vibrations
of ego, self-identity tenfold
with lots of eyes and vertebrates
watching, splashes and patterns,
mosaics of the Incas stare
from the wall like jungle gods
and goddesses.

A Carnival of Venice, the mask
and arms incarnation of new life
in Kolosov's search for self-identity,
Lina's "Nightbird" with its purple
knots and two hearts in love
like kites at a cocktail party
all shimmering off the wall,
a mixture of lipstick and highballs
greens and olives, lemons,
with oranges of red and Tantric love.

THE LOVE LETTER

after the painting by Vermeer

A highly personal
look inside.
A mistress with a lute
on a checkerboard floor.

As her servant
looks on approvingly
the mistress's pearl eyes
say: "What can it mean?"

A glimpse of the soul
in a narrow camera obscura
projected on our lens.
"What about me?"

A still note written
on paper, her mouth open
confounding the servant
with a smile to tell everything.

POST OFFICE

A perfect stillness, in chapel
the air rises like a carpet
from a blonde parquet floor
paneled small wood table
a place for a hat is all I need
where words belong at my elbow
I rest my arms on a ledge
a fulcrum where I can balance
on the tip of my pen, day begun
as I transcend the periods
that come between my thoughts.

So days might end in a letter
rearrangement of each
tiny atom that I breathe
motes of dust in eye beams
under the teardrop chandeliers
weeping crystals that hang
from a high ceiling as I write
a letter to send, put in a cage
where it will be sent away
to flutter among the eaves.

POSTA

In my Budapest neighborhood
where the *posta*'s wooden doors
magically open like a saloon
women in window cages
sort and stamp the mail
count out stamps colored red, yellow
green and blue for *forints*
as the door closes on my vacation.

I sit on a wooden bench
addressing postcards in stacks
turning over both sides, fitting
an address—stamps overflowing
words awaiting a final seal
of approval, imprimatur that like
a graceful bird helps cards fly
from my hand and out the windows.

NIGHT MAILMAN

At night, removing my mask
I walk the hallowed ground
under streetlights where I meet no one
past broken noses of lions
and swimming sea turtles across
the street, navigate the crosswalk
don't let the curbs trip me up
on the lawn of well-kept citizens
who keep secrets no one listens to
down alleys with long-legged shadows
where potholes don't follow
making sure I am always alone.

Make my rounds where no one's home,
a night mailman, nothing to deliver
in my close-mouthed pouch, skip
over addresses in my book, holding
cards no one sent, keeping track of
all dead letters that I will return
to be re-cased and re-sorted for
the living, unceremoniously
yet to be delivered, my sack is growing
my bag is aching, still I can't begin
to tell you of these words, forgotten.
What I couldn't find I carry with me
for another time when I'll return
after the daylight sounds.

SILENCE WAS DEAFENING

The silence was deafening when Joshua Bell
    played at the DC Metro station,
and no one stopped to listen to his Bach
    although it was backbreaking to play
underground to such an audience from
    Hell, all of them rushing to their next
connection, not to miss a "train" amidst
    what sounded like a jet engine's takeoff
his $3.5 million violin, a prop, and people
    stopping to throw in dollars to dust.

For forty-five minutes he gave his all
    to have people rush by him, no takers
stopped to listen, but a three-year-old boy
    pulled along by his mother in tow.
Meanwhile my internet speed has
    increased thanks to Xfinity, and I
will go on to send e-mails and receive
    junk mail as normal while the world
goes by and Joshua Bell continues
    to play, and no one will miss a beat.

COSMONAUTS

In the airways of the world
life awaits in jet streams at 33,000 feet
the blue radiant stratosphere resounds
with light and cruising flights of fields
crisscrossed in clouds—

Night rarely comes at all, but if
we close the screens of our eyes
trying to shut out the sun
that follows us, like day to night,
put our knees aside, stow our trays—

Pray for a Bailey's and a biscuit
try not to cough, adjust our headrests
swaddle in blankets, take in the whispering
sounds of compressed air, following
our in-flight ballistics path then—

Proceed as tiny dots adjust themselves
into the ping-pong game of space, our
"Ghost Riders in the Sky" written in contrails,
heads winking, blinking and nodding
as the earth turns us into satellites.

RADAR EYE

At 34,000 feet Keflavík on the radar screen
a mackerel-crossed sky—
like hands in the snow leave prints
tracings of contrails—overflowing
the ice shelves' margins

A continent—great glacial lakes
votive plains and plateaus
ridges of ice, we take a turn
toward Newfoundland,
the Northwest Territories,
vast swatches of space
open on the in-flight chessboard

To my radar eye, an uninhabited map
where dots keep moving,
to a place where wildfires went
unchecked, moved across Yellowknife.
Like a tracer bullet I follow our course
above the curvilinear earth towards
a vast horizon where Vancouver lies
off the far West Coast of my sight—

Then, before we dip to the south
with hours to the safe harbor
of Puget Sound, I see an airport
terminus, end of our map
that closes delivering us down the ramps
toward customs where I declare, I'm home.

CROSSING TO NOWHERE

In Kansas, a crossing to nowhere
a jurisdiction of dust and scarecrows
in cornfields in the open
where nothing in the world moves,
the hunters' words keep to themselves
in the muted mouths of crows
dust and disorder far as the eye can stare,
a target of bull's-eyes made from silos
threshers and wind farms,
the sprinklers kachew, kachew,
a mist made of sparrows
and sunflowers and overalls
that don't bust no matter
who wears them in or out in any kind
of weather, vain hope of rain
where the highways turn blue.

ROCK CARVINGS:
CHINESE RECONCILIATION SHRINE
TACOMA, WASHINGTON

*"Granite rock interprets the tragic
walk of the Chinese immigrants."*

My ear is washed
as a shell with the sound
of water that swirls
in its nautilus chamber.
How my head needs
solace from the tide
through the half-moon
of the bridge, curving
like the sound coming
in rivulets of words.

From across the grotto
where stones bleed
a confusion of tides
lapping at my feet
as we are swept up
the narrow passage
with a passion
the cars are shaking—
a configuration of stone.

As I offer a blessing
to empty boxcars
among the shadows
of men and women
swell of tides
that makes rings where
my words collect as

I toss my head, find
a spider inventing—
its web of meaning.

OTTO'S SONG

"Rain, rain, go away"

Otto sings his rain song
light in voice, soft and high
below my window, Otto's voice
a cheerful tune that rises
in its sweetness takes its cue
from the rain's light melody
of its peaceful voicing, note
by note in balance of the day
where it hangs its line, rising
one string at a time, a staff
whose life is not yet measured.

ELEVATOR

Outside the elevator, a lobby
of dingy rugs, a dark carpet
leaves its mark like carbon 14
while a pneumatic tube
sucks up mail through a vacuum
as I sit on a wrought iron chair
where rings of neon light
halo above me and bronze
doors open under terra-cotta pink
friezes of lions and gargoyles
and I feel like I'm in the maze
of the Minotaur where King Minos
lives and I hear what sounds
like a voice from the past tense
telling me not to go anywhere.

FIELDS OF COLOR

from the Marcio Díaz and William Song Exhibition at ArtXchange Gallery

Poppies awaken my eyes
see blue and white
in a wash of colors
like laundry hanging
on the lines of this poem.

Oranges like marbles
in acrylics, a black forest
stippled in green,
a rain forest of blues
in spring, patchworks

of butterfly wings, yellow
honeycombs of bees
and in soft hues, a meadow
of Shasta daisies
in strings of beads.

BIRTHDAY CARD

from Burk Ketchum

On a piece of shiny paper
freshly lacquered in acrylic
evergreens tower in mist
their spearmint limbs carrying
pine scent into the wind, flurries
of snow fall, cover the trees like
a candy wrapper rubbing off
on my fingertips, touch
of fresh pine needles
punctuates my skin; meanwhile
like a tattoo of dark ink its shadow
stippled on my shoulder
promises a silver future is
yet to come.

LIMBO

after the painting by Lisa West

In blue light ghosts move
like X-rays of themselves
with little halos in and out
of songs in dressing gowns
from the pause of waiting rooms.

Their faces like Cycladic sculptures
long ovoid faces without eyes
or mouths but narrow noses
move through bubbles made of circles
like they'd come from the Aegean.

Or Mediterranean, scribbled on blankets
names and numbers, a kind of
iconography of the living and dead
what metamorphosis is this that holds
us together roped and robed?

Here we are in soft watercolor
almost washed away, but on the
marble floor with masks of faces
come to save with the healing art
and the touchstones of saints.

Together ready to take our places
a frozen choreography out of a chorus
line made from a choric ode
that we say in monologue like
Gregorian chants to ourselves.

EXHIBITION IN BUDAPEST, SZÉPMŰVÉSZETI MÚZEUM

The man and woman so dappled by sunlight
their bodies are like fireflies, and a little girl
whose hands are stanzas interlocked like poems.

Nearby, a man looks on, his beard part of the tree
with bark growing in the background, while
the green and verdant forest seems a garnish.

The ground scatters minnows of light which
seem to run around them like a reflecting pool
and the swing in their hands, a lifeline to pull

the couple back from floating away into the sun
as they hold it while blue ribbons rise on the woman
to cover her dress like a butterfly bush.

Everyone seems transfixed for a moment—
while we observe straw hats and hair seeming
to alight like moths in air.

The painting seems to hover above our feet,
while we hold steady just to look and try
to keep from walking into it.

GOLD MEDAL

"We'll always have Paris."
      —Rick in <u>Casablanca</u>

After the dirty Seine rolled by
the volleyball courts under the Eiffel Tower
and the medals had been put to bed
sleeping better than the athletes did
at shabby St. Denis. They'll always be
a diver, Marchand with a golden smile
to cheer, the Marathon finish, mile after mile
down the tree-lined streets of the Champs
along the path where women walked to
declare the rights of man in front of the Conciergerie
where Lokedi locked in the lead until Hassan
crossed the bleu finish line for Netherlands
in orange, white and green in the final race
where everyone wins.

SUMMER IS LIGHT TO THE TOUCH

As I dangle my toes
in the gene pool wondering
what I will come up with

at the end of my bait, a hook
to catch what wriggles away
a flashy thing called love.

I lure with words what swims
around me, everything in the air
I can't divine without my rod.

I know it's just waiting there—
unbidden, if I can trust—wait
long enough to keep quiet.

SHINY THINGS

Monday, I'm at Cosmonaut Café
among the reggae sounds of metal clanging
like a garage in Gasoline Alley
as Jan makes espresso from a sarcophagus
of a coffee machine where he is bending
his arm to pull another shot, shiny metallic glow.

We're among cosmonauts, photos of
Valentina Tereshkova, first female astronaut in space,
rhymes vaguely with "Sinatra" where
I'm tucked into the corner booth riveted
into a metal contraption for a table
bolted into the wall, eating Red Hots.

Looking at rubles under glass, shiny as koi
swimming in slow-motion in a silver pond,
light catching their tails while I gently rock
to the shiny bait of reggae music drumming
its way into my head, metallic threads
of my jeans holding onto this day.

Emotional zip ties run deep this morning
all the way to my silver earring's stud
bright shiny things still remain
from a former wife and life, while I am riveted
to a reverie where I, too, am shining
in this current that carries me into space.

ACKNOWLEDGMENTS

The author thanks and acknowledges the publications and venues where poems in this collection previously appeared:

Aria: "Night Mailman"

Blue Poppy: "Song for a Young Male Townsend's Warbler"

The Bluebird Word: "Golden-Crowned Kinglets"

Budapest After Dark: "Posta," "The Lighted Bridges of Budapest," "Fiumei Cemetery," "Sadie and Her Scissors," "Radar Eye"

Jack Straw Productions: "Budapest After Dark"

Kingfisher Poetry Forum 2: "Holding On in Irpin, Ukraine," "Will Sheep Safely Graze," "Eventide"

Listener's Notes KUOW FM: "Voice in the Machine"

The Nature of Our Times: "Online Gallery," "On Humans"

Poets for Human Rights, National Poetry Month, 2024: "Mille Fiori"

Purr and Yowl: An Anthology of Poetry About Cats: "Dorian Grey," "Mr. Cannoli, Calico Cat"

Sailor's Review #22: "I Hugged the Brandenburg Concerto #2"

Windblown: "Twin Harbor's State Park Near Grayland," "Naches Tavern"

ABOUT THE AUTHOR

Michael Magee has lived in England and his poems have been heard and read on BBC1, at Shakespeare and Company, Paris, San Francisco's Dancing Poetry Contest and on Writer's Almanac and VerseDaily.org. He recently read at Jack Straw Studios in Seattle and at the AWP in Seattle. He is the author of *Penny Princess: a child's coloring book* and three travel chapbooks: *Self-Variations on Greece and Turkey*; *Ireland's Eye*; and *Vanishing Points: Ghost Towns of the West*. His chapbook *Love is a Blur* is on the subject of dementia and is dedicated to his late wife, Jean.

While in England his play *A Night in Reading Gaol with Oscar Wilde* was produced in Derby, and *Shank's Mare* was made into a movie at the Bare Bones: Script to Screen Film Festival in Tulsa, Oklahoma. His chapbook *Budapest After Dark* was published by Open Sesame Books in 2024. His work has also appeared in *Poetry* (Chicago), *Epoch*, *Poetry Northwest* (the original), *PoetryAtlas.org*, *Raven Chronicles*, and *Cirque*. He has recently travelled to Budapest, Hungary, and lives in Tacoma, Washington.